Content-Based Instruction

Margo DelliCarpini and Orlando B. Alonso

English
Language
Teacher
Development
Series

Thomas S. C. Farrell,
Series Editor

Typeset in Janson and Frutiger
by Capitol Communications, LLC, Crofton, Maryland USA
and printed by Gasch Printing, LLC, Odenton, Maryland USA

TESOL International Association
1925 Ballenger Avenue
Alexandria, Virginia 22314 USA
Tel 703-836-0774 • Fax 703-836-7864

Publishing Manager: Carol Edwards
Cover Design: Tomiko Breland
Copyeditor: Jean House

TESOL Book Publications Committee
John I. Liontas, Chair

Maureen S. Andrade	Joe McVeigh
Jennifer Lebedev	Gail Schafers
Robyn L. Brinks Lockwood	Lynn Zimmerman

Project overview: John I. Liontas and Robyn L. Brinks Lockwood
Reviewer: Soonyoung Hwang An

ISBN 9781942223115

Contents

About the Authors

Margo DelliCarpini is TESOL Professor and Chair of the Department of Middle and High School Education at Lehman College, City University of New York, USA. Her current research focuses on two-way CBI (content-based instruction) and collaboration between educators of TESOL and STEM (science, technology, engineering, and mathematics).

Orlando B. Alonso is a Mathematics Education Professor and Co-coordinator of the Mathematics Education Program at Lehman College, City University of New York, USA. His research interests include combinatorial geometry, mathematics education, and teacher collaboration between mathematics and TESOL educators.

Series Editor's Preface

The English Language Teacher Development (ELTD) Series consists of a set of short resource books for English language teachers that are written in a jargon-free and accessible manner for all types of teachers of English (native and nonnative speakers of English, experienced and novice teachers). The ELTD Series is designed to offer teachers a theory-to-practice approach to English language teaching, and each book offers a wide variety of practical teaching approaches and methods for the topic at hand. Each book also offers opportunities for teachers to interact with the materials presented. The books can be used in preservice settings or in-service courses and by individuals looking for ways to refresh their practice.

Margo DelliCarpini and Orlando Alonso's book *Content-Based Instruction* explores different approaches to teaching content-based instruction (CBI) in the English language classroom. They provide a comprehensive overview of how to teach CBI in an easy-to-follow guide that language teachers will find very practical for their own contexts. Topics covered include academic language development challenges and approaches, interdisciplinary teacher collaboration, and a two-way approach to CBI where content teachers and English language teachers work together and collaboratively develop complementary content-driven and language-driven CBI objectives. *Content Based Instruction* is a valuable addition to the literature in our profession.

I am very grateful to the authors who contributed to the ELTD Series for sharing their knowledge and expertise with other TESOL professionals because they have done so willingly and without any compensation to make these short books affordable to language teachers throughout the world. It was truly an honor for me to work with each of these authors as they selflessly gave up their valuable time for the advancement of TESOL.

Thomas S. C. Farrell

1

Introduction

Use of English as an academic lingua franca continues to expand to settings around the globe, and it has become a primary language of higher education in many locations (Mauranen, 2003). English-medium programs have expanded internationally, increasing the number of students studying within an English language framework (Coleman, 2006). Although the expectation for programs in countries such as Australia, Canada, the United Kingdom, and the United States is to provide instruction in English, increasing numbers of institutions located in countries where English is not the native language are offering courses and whole programs in English (Brandt, 2010). Graddol (2007, p. 74) discusses that with almost 66% of the top 100 universities worldwide in English-speaking countries, the result is increased pressure on institutions globally to provide English-medium programs.

Taking the United States and Canada, with their large English language learner (ELL) populations as examples, it is evident that academic success for secondary-level ELLs has been problematic. Recent research reveals that only 54% of secondary-level ELLs in Alberta, Canada, complete school, as opposed to 70% of native-English-speaking students (Derwing, DeCorby, Ichikawa, & Jamieson, 1999). In the United States, which has one of the largest global ELL populations, academic achievement for these students is no less challenging. According to Richard Fry (2007), of the Pew Hispanic Center, ELLs are "much less likely than other students to score at or above proficient levels in both mathematics and reading/language arts" (¶ 4). Although not all ELLs struggle with academic performance, national assessments reveal that, as a group, these students are not performing at the same level as their native-speaking counterparts.

These factors make the meaningful and successful integration of content and language critical for student success in a variety of secondary and higher educational settings. Content-based instruction (CBI), the prevalent method of instruction in English language programs globally (referred to as content- and language-integrated learning, or CLIL), can address this need. English language teaching professionals whose primary role has been to develop language skills may be underprepared to work with the actual content of CBI, however. English language teaching content consists of linguistics, applied linguistics, and language pedagogy. English language teachers may struggle with the demands of the academic content in which they are required to build academic language skills, which can cause the unintended problem of not adequately contributing to developing the skills needed for success in the content subject and not developing the language skills associated with academic language. English language teachers may select the content to teach based on their strengths or student interests and lack awareness and understanding of the needs of ELLs in the mainstream classroom.

Conversely, content teachers might underestimate the interconnections between language development and achievement in the subject matter. Investigations of content teacher preparation in the United States report that 77% of content-area teachers have had no coursework or professional development addressing ELLs (National Center for Educational Statistics, 2002), and in a survey of seven states in the United States, less than 8% of content teachers who work with ELLs reported having participated in 8 or more hours of professional development specifically relating to ELLs (National Center for Educational Statistics, 2002). This is a critical challenge because a number of efforts both in the United States and other educational settings have created a situation in which more and more ELLs are in English immersion contexts yet do not have access to bilingual education or high-quality English language services. de Jong and Harper (2005) point out that the "extraordinary language and literacy demands remain invisible" in the academic classroom (p. 102).

English language teachers must focus not only on developing students' language skills but on content in a way that will foster success in mainstream, subject-area classrooms and for academic success in English-medium settings in secondary and higher educational settings. Content teachers, on the other hand, are left to focus on the content, which is appropriate, but are unaware of how to make the language of the discipline visible so that ELLs have access to the content.

This book discusses traditional definitions of CBI and how those must be modified to address the changing needs, demographics, and expectations for those who teach English as a second, foreign, or additional language as well as those teaching English for academic purposes and English for specific purposes. Focusing on content and English language teaching partnerships, we discuss the importance and challenge of developing authentic academic language. The designed paired complementary activities presented in this book aim to meet the need for English language students to be successful in academic content areas, focusing on students' development of the language of the discipline and related social language in both settings through effective collaboration and two-way CBI.

Activity 1

Identify one major challenge or obstacle that ELLs face in developing each of the four skills in the content classroom, specifically focusing on academic language skills. Brainstorm a possible solution to your identified challenge or obstacle. Finally, how could your proposed solution be actualized in both the content and language classroom? Fill out Table 1.

Table 1. Brainstorming Activity 1

Language skill	Challenge	Possible solution	Actualization in the content setting	Actualization in the language setting
Reading				
Writing				
Listening				
Speaking				

REFLECTIVE BREAK

- As an English language teacher, what is your level of preparation of and experience with subjects beyond those included in your English language teacher preparation program?

- As a content teacher, what is your level of preparation of and experience working with ELLs in your content classroom?

  — What challenges do you face as an educator in developing the academic language skills of the students you teach?

  — What have your observations been regarding ELLs in content classes and English-medium environments?

Keeping Up With the Times

What Is CBI?

Brinton, Snow, and Wesche (1989) define CBI as "the integration of content with language-teaching aims" (p. 2). This definition generally provides for the integration of some content within the goals of the language program. The content can be selected based on teacher interests, student interests, or program needs and often is selected based on a combination of these factors. In subsequent discussions of the content of CBI, Crandall and Tucker (1990) define it as "an approach to language instruction that integrates the presentation of topics or tasks from subject-matter classes (e.g., math, social studies) within the context of teaching a second or foreign language" (p. 187). These two definitions focus on instruction taking place in the language classroom and the use of some academic subject matter as the vehicle for language learning.

With the increased demands for the development of academic language within the context of an academic, English-medium program, the content in CBI needs to be carefully considered. Recently, TESOL International Association (2008) provided this updated definition of CBI: "As contrasted with language teaching in isolation, CBI uses specific subject matter on which to base language instruction. In other words, the language is taught within the context of a specific academic subject" (p. 1). This definition does not distinguish between the provision of these services taking place in the English language or subject-area classroom, but it does squarely place CBI within the context of a specific academic subject.

CBI enhances the acquisition of both language and content, in either the language or content classroom. CBI is based on theories of second language (L2) acquisition, and research suggests that this approach is effective in developing both language proficiency and content knowledge for ELLs in a number of diverse educational settings (Grabe & Stoller, 1997; Short, Echevarría, & Richards-Tutor, 2011).

ELLs can face a number of challenges in the mainstream content classroom. Academic English, especially in complex and technical subjects, is frequently very different from the types of communicative language teachers traditionally strive to develop in a communicative language-learning environment, so the successful integration of language and content is necessary for the development of the types of language ELLs need to master in their academic settings.

Approaches to CBI

CBI can be either content driven or language driven (Met, 1999). In a content-driven approach, content is presented and taught in English. Learning content is the primary goal, and learning English is a secondary goal. The content objectives are driven by the larger curricular goals, and teachers must select language objectives in conjunction with these content objectives. Students are assessed on their mastery of the content, rather than on language gains. Language-driven CBI, on the other hand (again summarizing Met, 1999), is the mirror image of content-driven CBI. In this framework the content is used to learn English, and learning the language is a priority. Learning the content is not purposeful and occurs as a consequence of the focus on language within a particular content area. The language objectives are driven by the language (not content) curricular demands and students are assessed based on gains in language proficiency, not directly on content learning.

Even though CBI can be implemented in either the content or English language classroom, to date, most of the practice that occurs, regardless of the approach and whether content-driven or language-driven, does so in the English language classroom exclusively. Mainstream content teachers are often unprepared or underprepared to work with ELLs in their classrooms, especially at the secondary school level. This is an important point because many settings (e.g., in Canada and Europe) are moving toward immersion, either manifested as CBI or CLIL, which is an extension of CBI philosophy.

CBI is manifested globally in a number of ways, including but not limited to sheltered instruction, cognitive academic language learning approach (CALLA), sheltered instruction observation protocol (SIOP), CLIL, and immersion education in Canada (see Table 2 for an overview). Both CLIL and immersion language education in Canada focus on the simultaneous development of language and content, and immersion education can be complete immersion (English-only or partial, where two languages are taught simultaneously (e.g., French and English) with students from both first language (L1) groups learning together (dual-language education in the United States). Canadian

Table 2. Prevalent Methods of CBI

Feature	Advantages	Disadvantages
CALLA: Cognitive Academic Language Learning Approach		
–Based on cognitive learning theories –Five main components: prepare, present, practice, evaluate, expand –Hands-on, inquiry-based learning –Can be implemented in English language and bilingual education settings –Taught by English language teachers	–Places value on students' prior knowledge –Develops a meta-cognitive awareness of language learning –Strategies are selected that meet students' language and content learning needs –Successful development of cooperative learning skills –Enhances student motivation –Appropriate for all instructional and language proficiency levels	–No input or collaboration from content- or subject-area teachers required –Content may be aligned with the greater curriculum, but it may be teacher selected and not aligned

(Continued on p. 8)

Table 2. *(continued)*

Feature	Advantages	Disadvantages
SIOP: Sheltered Instruction Observation Protocol		
–Scientifically validated –Eight main components: lesson preparation, building background, comprehensible input, strategies, interaction, practice and application; lesson delivery, review, and assessment –Within main components are 30 subfeatures –Can be used in English language and content settings	–Language and content objectives in each lesson –Potential to develop academic language –Integration of language and content –May benefit both ELLs and native English-speaking students in the same classroom –Appropriate for all instructional and language proficiency levels	–Can be used in subject-area classrooms, but frequently implemented only in English language teaching settings –No collaboration between content and English language teachers results in lack of knowledge about language pedagogy for content teachers and lack of knowledge about the content for English language teachers
CLIL: Content- and Language-Integrated Learning		
–Ranges from the soft form (English language teaching CLIL) to the hard form (content-focused CLIL) – Coyle's 4 *C*s are essential elements: **c**ontent, **c**ommunication, **c**ognition, **c**ulture –PAR framework: preparation; reasoning activities; review –Usually English medium but has been applied to other language settings such as Spanish and Basque –Requires collaboration or co-teaching between language and subject teacher	–Students are involved in conceptual tasks –Fully integrated language and content –Fosters meaningful communication –Natural use of the target language –Increases students' motivation and confidence in both language and content –Appropriate for all instructional and language proficiency levels	–Language teachers' lack of content knowledge –Content teachers' lack of knowledge about language pedagogy –Language instruction may be pushed to the side to spend more time on the content –Teachers may have unsuccessful experiences co-teaching and collaborating and may have little support in doing so

(Continued on p. 9)

Table 2. *(continued)*

Feature	Advantages	Disadvantages
ESP: English for Specific Purposes		
–Focused on preparing students in English specific to a particular profession or occupation –Learner centered: Decisions about content and strategies based on learners' specific needs –Language taught is based on the language demands of the specific field –Makes use of the methodology and activities of the specific discipline. –English language settings –Can include English for academic purposes (EAP)	–Learner centered –Relevant topics to meet students' immediate needs –Can include vocational, professional, and academic purposes –Flexible content and methodologies –Builds learner autonomy	–Mostly appropriate for intermediate to advanced learners –Assumes basic knowledge of the target language –May not focus enough on some language skills (e.g., focus on reading rather than speaking)

(Continued on p. 10)

immersion programs have become a model worldwide because of their success in building students' language, literacy, and academic skills regardless of the L1. Research has consistently found that students in these language immersion programs generally achieve higher levels of proficiency in all areas compared to monolingual students in monolingual programs (Genesee, 2004).

These models share similarities but have subtly different approaches to language and content learning. Sheltered instruction attempts to make the content accessible to ELLs, and in a true sheltered model, subject-area teachers provide instruction; frequently, this takes place in the language classroom and is taught by language teachers. Many of these programs can be bilingual or monolingual in nature.

Table 2. *(continued)*

Feature	Advantages	Disadvantages
Immersion Programs		
–Students are immersed in the language program throughout the school day –Total immersion: 100% of instruction is in the target language –Partial immersion: 50% target language/50% native language instruction but can vary in the L2 emphasis –Dual immersion: L1 and L2 learners are grouped together –Regular school curriculum taught through target language	–Immersion programs can be for early entry (5–6 years of age), middle immersion (9–10 years of age), late immersion (11–14 years of age) –Simultaneous acquisition of language and content –Highly effective in developing both language and content –Stronger literacy skills are developed in both the L1 and L2, especially with early immersion programs	–Total immersion may not be favored by some families or school settings –Highly qualified immersion teachers may be in short supply –Partial immersion generally not as effective as total immersion but more prevalent. May require two teachers (one fluent in the L1 and the other in the L2, if a bilingual teacher is not available) –Late immersion students who do not have strong L1 literacy skills and interrupted formal education may struggle with the academic language requirements

These approaches are similar in that they focus on the subject, or content area, as the vehicle for language instruction, rather than explicit, decontextualized language teaching. Essentially, these approaches fall within three main models of CBI: the sheltered model, the adjunct model, and the theme-based model (Brinton, Snow, & Wesche, 1989). Although similar, each of these models provides a variation on CBI (see Table 3). These models fall under the umbrella of CBI; however, there are differences in how they are actualized in the classroom. The *sheltered model* features content or subject courses being taught in the target language using strategies that scaffold language

Table 3. Models of CBI

Contextual Factors	Advantages	Disadvantages
Sheltered Model		
–Prevalent in English L1 settings –Frequently implemented in elementary and secondary educational settings	–ELLs acquire the same content knowledge as native-speaking students –Language development is seen as a consequence of content learning in an authentic setting –Scaffolding of academic language –May be either content driven or language driven	–Subject-area teachers may not have adequate preparation in working with ELLs –English language teachers may not have the requisite content knowledge needed to effectively build the skills needed for success in the content classroom –Little actual collaboration between English language teachers and content teachers –Content may be selected based on teacher interest rather than on academic demands
Adjunct Model (also referred to as the *Linked Model*)		
–Prevalent in L2 contexts –Offered in English-medium institutions –Academic in nature	–Language and content courses are linked –Courses are (ideally) developed by both language and content specialists –Both courses share a common content base, but the approach differs between the language and content course –Ideal for collaboration between English language teachers and content teachers	–Requires a great deal of planning –English language teachers may be marginalized by the content teacher, who may view himself or herself as the real teacher (positioning)

(Continued on p. 12)

Table 3. *(continued)*

Contextual Factors	Advantages	Disadvantages
Theme-Based Model		
–Prevalent in higher education and adult educational settings – Commonly offered in foreign language learning contexts –Recognized by many as traditional English language instruction	–Most easily implemented –Themes usually selected based on student interest and needs of learners –Highly student centered –Language learning objectives usually take precedence over content learning objectives (language driven)	–English language teacher operates independently and often in isolation from other content- or subject-area teachers –Frequently taught by English language teachers in standalone English language programs that have academic language requirements –Actual content learning may not occur

in a way that makes the content accessible to ELLs. The sheltered approach is frequently found in immersion settings, and instruction is provided by a subject-area specialist (not a professional English language teacher). This is considered a content-driven approach because the learning of the subject matter is the primary goal. Students are assessed on their mastery of the content material.

In the *adjunct model*, the goal is the development of both language and subject matter learning. In such a model, students advance in language proficiency and acquire content knowledge simultaneously, frequently working with both language and content teachers. Assessment of both is a feature. Language teachers are responsible for the language instruction, and subject-area specialists are responsible for the content instruction. The *adjunct model* ideally features co-teaching by both the subject and language specialist. The true adjunct model would be both language driven and content driven.

Finally, in the *theme-based model* of CBI, the goal is language development. The themes, or content, are selected by the teacher or based on student needs and interests. Assessment is based on gains of language proficiency, and content learning is a result of the focus of the theme but is not the primary goal of instruction. The instructors are language educators, and the theme-based model is a language-driven approach to CBI.

Grabe and Stoller (1997) offer the following rationale for CBI: First, in classrooms where content is the focus, students are exposed to a linguistically rich environment while the English language teacher is attending to language learning needs. The content (ideally) is linked to their lives, and to prior learning and is relevant to their needs. Grabe and Stoller (1997) discuss how the content of CBI is engaging to learners. Contextualized learning, where language is developed that is useful in the students' setting, is an objective of effective CBI. Rather than treating language as a subject, students are given the opportunity to explore topics that are interesting during lessons that have been specifically developed to address both content and language learning. Therefore, authentic language development is a consequence of content learning. In an effective CBI setting, language teachers make language learning explicit but relevant. In other words, students are not exposed to decontextualized language drills but are authentically engaged in tasks that promote language acquisition. If these courses are structured properly, students are able to build on their prior language learning experiences to develop higher levels of proficiency. The information presented in CBI should be cognitively demanding, therefore increasing students' intrinsic motivation. Additionally, CBI is flexible in terms of strategies and student-centered activities that can support both the acquisition of language skills and the development of subject-area understandings.

The Challenge of Effective CBI

Despite the promise of CBI, many English language teachers struggle with the selection of content that is aligned with the program's academic curriculum, and often have had little preparation in the academic subject they are working with. Conversely, the subject teacher often has had little preparation in language pedagogy and is underprepared to actually meet the linguistic needs of language learners in the subject-area classroom. In all CBI settings, both English language teachers and subject teachers may not know how to build academic language because there may be little actual understanding of the role language plays in content learning for subject-area teachers. In CLIL settings, for example, the co-teaching aspect may be a challenge because there may be little understanding of how to effectively co-teach (we discuss effective collaboration for successful two-way CBI in Chapter 5); therefore, implementing these approaches in isolation becomes the default. Mehisto (2008) found that CLIL classes taught only by content teachers provided L2 support mostly through translation. This research also found that the actual practice of team teaching was the biggest drawback to successful CLIL, and this finding is supported by other related research (Mehisto, Marsh, & Frigols, 2008). These challenges to effective CBI are present not only in teachers' co-teaching skills and in knowledge of the required content and language pedagogy. As Snow (1998) suggests, the major challenge lies in the actual relationship between language and content, and regardless of teachers' skills in their disciplines, "not all the teachers are prepared to focus on content and language goals" (Mehisto, Marsh, & Frigols, 2008, p. 21).

To best serve ELLs and prepare them for academic success, CBI must be re-imagined to include an expanded notion of the role that the English language teacher plays in building academic language, and the role and responsibility of the content- or subject-area teacher must be examined and redefined to include the responsibility of making the language of the discipline visible in the mainstream-subject classroom so that ELLs have access to the material and opportunities for success.

Activity 2

Using Table 3 as a starting point for filling out Table 4, first brainstorm any approaches you are aware of that fall under these three models. Then list additional advantages and disadvantages to the models described based on your experiences. Finally, in the last row in Table 4, describe the model or approach in your teaching setting or the model or approach with which you have experience (theoretical or practical) as a result of your teacher preparation or professional development opportunities.

Table 4. Brainstorming Activity 2

Model	Examples	Features	
		Advantages	Disadvantages
Sheltered Model			
Adjunct Model (also referred to as the *Linked Model*)			
Theme-Based Model			
My Model or Approach			

REFLECTIVE BREAK

- How must traditional notions of CBI be redefined to address the needs of ELLs regarding the development of both academic language and content knowledge?

- What challenges might English language teachers and mainstream mathematics teachers face in implementing either language-driven or content-driven CBI in their classrooms?

- How can TESOL's definition of CBI be interpreted for teachers in both the language and the content classroom?

3

Developing Academic Language

Challenges of Academic Language Learning

The development of academic language skills in a L2 can be difficult, and research indicates that ELLs face multiple challenges in developing the academic skills in English needed for success in North American school settings (Herrera & Murray, 2005). As stated in the Introduction, secondary-level ELLs in Canada and the United States are not performing at the same level as their native-speaking counterparts in terms of academic achievement on standardized assessments. In fact, in 2008 the Toronto District School Board, which is the largest and most linguistically diverse district in Canada, identified all kindergarten ELLs as at-risk because of the significant achievement gap that exists academically between ELLs in general and their native-English-speaking counterparts (McGloin, 2011; Toronto District School Board, 2008). This is a result of increasing diversity in the ELL population as well as an increased focus on local and national assessments in English coupled with decreasing accommodations for students whose native language differs from that of the assessment. Although global data for English language at the higher educational level and in secondary-level English-medium programs is not easily accessible, it is possible to draw the conclusion that the development of English for academic purposes in these settings is not easily attainable. One source of evidence that we draw on to support this claim is the disparity of academic publications between native- and nonnative-English-speaking scholars. Although the vast majority of indexed publications are published in English, international scholars publishing in English are grossly underrepresented (King, 2004). One reason for this disproportionate representation is the English proficiency levels of the scholars (Man, Weinkaif, Tsang, & Sin, 2004).

An Academic Subject in Detail: The Language of Mathematics

This chapter focuses on the language of mathematics for a number of reasons. First, globally, academic English programs tend to focus on science, technology, engineering, and mathematics (STEM) subjects and many international students are funded in their university endeavors if they are pursuing degrees in STEM fields. Second, scientific publishing is an important part of international scholarship and provides vast funding opportunities for research, but only 31 countries out of 191 contribute to this research (King, 2004), which is overwhelmingly published in English, with the United States and the United Kingdom ranking first and second, respectively, in terms of global citation analysis (King, 2004). Finally, STEM subjects are increasingly focused on in countries such as the United States in response to increased demands for leadership in these areas internationally. The language of mathematics underlies these fields.

It is often falsely assumed that math is an international language, and therefore the language of mathematics may be underfocused in the English language classroom. Another false assumption is the notion that math consists of numbers, and knowledge of numbers is enough. Both of these *math myths* are false. The language of math is highly complex and can pose a number of linguistic challenges for ELLs. Math is highly communicative; it requires students to be fluent in the language of mathematics to build conceptual knowledge, and it requires a high level of literacy to comprehend explanations, directions, and word problems. The linguistic challenges ELLs face encompass almost all of what is considered in language learning. Martiniello (2008, p. 176) reports that the following features and linguistic patterns cause difficulty for ELLs on math assessments:

- syntactic—multiclausal complex structures with embedded adverbial and relative clauses, long phrases with embedded noun and prepositional phrases, lack of clear relationships between the syntactic units;

- lexical—unfamiliar vocabulary, high-frequency words usually learned at home and not in school, polysemous or multiple-meaning words;

- references to mainstream U.S. culture;

- test or text layout—lack of one-to-one correspondence between the syntactic boundaries of clauses and the layout of the text in the printed test

In addition to these linguistic challenges, ELLs must overcome gaps in cultural knowledge, as mathematics word problems frequently include events and activities that may be culturally situated. ELLs must also be able to comprehend the symbolic language of mathematics, associate the mathematical symbols and notation to concepts, and then have the requisite vocabulary and language skills to discuss, describe, analyze, solve problems and rote mathematical exercises, justify, and develop arguments and informal or formal proofs. For example, the understanding that the symbol $\sqrt{}$ (radical sign) means *the square root of* and that a square root of a number b (b is called the *radicand*) [$\sqrt{b}$] is a number that when squared gives the number b, and then be able to solve an equation using the square root. The symbol $\sqrt{}$ carries a great deal of meaning and requires a deep level of understanding of complex mathematical concepts.

Application to Academic Language Across Disciplines

Although the preceding discussion focuses on the language of mathematics because math underlies STEM subjects, it can be applied to all content areas. Each subject has unique ways of making meaning, orally and in writing, and unique ways of communicating and interpreting the discourse of the discipline. Martiniello's (2008) findings on the linguistic complexity of text features in mathematics can apply across the content areas, and by focusing attention on the linguistic complexities inherent in subject-area discourse, one can begin to deconstruct the language of the discipline. Language is an important pedagogical tool. The development of appropriate academic language is critical for all learners, but ELLs have unique needs of which teachers in the classroom must be aware. The types of language needed to gain academic mastery lend themselves not only to the development of content knowledge, but to the development of language in general.

Activity 3

Select a problem or problems from the subject-area material that your students must master. Using Table 5, identify the linguistic features that can cause difficulty for ELLs and the nature of the difficulty. Finally, identify a possible solution to this problem.

Table 5. Brainstorming Activity 3

Feature	Challenge	Possible solution
Syntax		
Vocabulary		
Cultural issues		
Text and text layout		
Idiomatic use of language		

Reflective Break

- What preparation have you received to enable you to engage in either CBI (for English language teachers) or sheltered instruction (for content teachers)? Was this preparation adequate?

- What challenges have you faced in developing the academic language of ELLs for success in their content classrooms?

- How can English language and content teachers learn about each other's disciplines and become aware of the needs of ELLs in the mainstream classroom or the actual requirements of the content area?

4

Interdisciplinary Teacher Collaboration

It may seem apparent that any form of CBI, to be effective, requires collaborative practice between English language teachers and subject-area teachers. Such collaboration is rare, however, and when it does occur may not be effective in meeting the desired goals. This chapter discusses how to develop effective collaborative partnerships and provides an overview of collaboration that makes room for a number of different teaching contexts.

One of the main challenges in the effective implementation of CBI, regardless of the form it takes, is that content teachers are not language teachers, and language teachers do not necessarily have backgrounds in mathematics, history, sciences, or literature. The factors related to teacher preparation can result in ELLs not receiving adequate instruction in either setting (if actual content learning is the goal, in addition to language learning) despite the best efforts and intentions of both sets of teachers.

Even if English language teachers and content teachers both receive adequate preparation in content and language pedagogy, the needs of ELLs still may not be met. Research indicates that content-area teachers feel that it is not their responsibility to develop ELLs' language skills, and that the professional organizations that shape the standards and expectations for content education often fail to include ELLs in the discussion (de Jong & Harper, 2005). Conversely, if English language teachers have adequate subject-area background, which is rare and difficult considering the number of different subject areas ELLs need to gain mastery in, the actual content focused on may not be aligned to what is being taught in the mainstream subject-area classroom. This may result in development of academic language skills for ELLs but may not adequately prepare them for success in the actual secondary-level, mainstream content classroom.

One way to address the logical problem of CBI is through teacher collaboration and a two-way approach to CBI (discussed in Chapter 5).

What Is Teacher Collaboration?

Teacher collaboration refers to activities ranging from informal discussions about shared students to highly structured and formalized co-teaching models. We see collaboration, therefore, as a continuum, and we define formal co-teaching as the *strong form* of collaborative practice. We define the informal discussions that can take place over lunch or in the hallway the *weak form* of collaboration. Practices that fall in the middle of these extremes can include co-planning lessons, sharing lesson plans and materials, professional visits to each other's classroom, expert consultations (where a content teacher observes the English language teacher and offers feedback on how more content knowledge might be built in, and where the English language teacher observes the mathematics or science class and offers feedback on how language learning can be integrated). Both forms, and the practices that fall in between, offer mainstream and English language teachers a way to address the needs of ELLs within both the mainstream and English language classrooms. Figure 1 further demonstrates the continuum of collaborative practices.

We believe that it is necessary for English language teachers and subject-area teachers to engage in collaborative practices that enhance

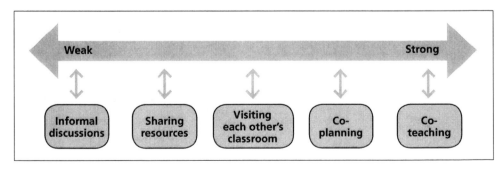

Figure 1. Continuum of Collaborative Practices

CBI in both the mainstream and English language setting. Any of the practices, or a combination, can be effective. Co-teaching, what we call the strong form of collaboration, is the most challenging due to programmatic factors, relationship between the parties, and positioning of the English language teacher in relation to the subject-area teacher (English language teachers are often marginalized and seen as less than real teachers), and general logistical issues. When the barriers that can and do exist in co-teaching relationships are overcome, however, this can be the most successful and enriching way to collaborate for both teachers and students. We speak from our own experiences as a co-teaching partnership. Table 6 shows some of the prevalent co-teaching models and how these might look in the English language classroom.

Why Collaborate?

When reviewing the literature, the evidence suggests that ELLs and their teachers benefit when collaborative practices exist. The benefits to teachers include increased partnership and reduced isolation, increased efficiency and effectiveness, ability to share responsibilities of teaching, enhanced ability to reflect on practice and to learn from colleagues, and opportunity to engage in a continuous improvement cycle

Table 6. Co-Teaching Models

Features (Friend & Cook, 2003)	ELL/content applications (Honigsfeld & Dove, 2008, p. 9)
One Teaching, One Drifting	
−One teacher plans and instructs, and one teacher provides adaptations and other support as needed −Requires very little joint planning −Should be used sparingly −Can result in one teacher, most often the general educator, taking the lead role the majority of the time −Can also be distracting to students, especially those who may become dependent on the drifting teacher	Mainstream and English language teacher take turns assuming the lead role while the other teaches on purpose. This allows both teachers to give minilessons (1–5 minutes) to individuals or small groups of students. Teaching on purpose can focus on a language or content concept or skill.

(Continued on p. 24)

Table 6. *(continued)*

Features (Friend & Cook, 2003)	ELL/content applications (Honigsfeld & Dove, 2008, p. 9)
Parallel Teaching	
–Teachers share responsibility for planning and instruction –Class is split into heterogeneous groups, and each teacher instructs half on the same material –Content covered is the same, but methods of delivery may differ –Both teachers need to be proficient in the content being taught	Students are grouped hetero-geneously. Each teacher works with one of the groups. Smaller groups allow ELLs to experience additional opportunities for interaction and teacher feedback.
Station Teaching	
–Teachers divide the responsibility of planning and instruction –Students rotate on a predetermined schedule through stations –Teachers repeat instruction to each group that comes through; delivery may vary according to student needs –Approach can be used even if teachers have very different pedagogical approaches –Each teacher instructs every student	Multiple groups of students who work on specific skills either for the whole class or rotate from station to station allow teachers to facilitate and monitor student work. Learning centers can target specific language and content needs, and differentiation of content, process, and product can occur.
Alternative Teaching	
–Teachers divide responsibilities for planning and instruction –The majority of students remain in a large-group setting, but some students work in a small group for preteaching, enrichment, reteaching, or other individualized instruction –Approach allows for highly individualized instruction –Teachers should be careful that the same students are not always pulled aside	Students are flexibly grouped according to assigned language proficiency levels, knowledge, skills, etc. These groupings are temporary and change with the topic or skill under investigation.

(Continued on p. 25)

Table 6. *(continued)*

Features (Friend & Cook, 2003)	ELL/content applications (Honigsfeld & Dove, 2008, p. 9)
Team Teaching	
−Teachers share responsibilities for planning and instruction −Teachers work as a team to introduce new content, work on developing skills, clarify information, and facilitate learning and classroom management −This requires the most mutual trust and respect between teachers and requires that they be able to mesh their teaching styles	Both teachers are directing the whole group; teachers work cooperatively and teach the same lesson at the same time. For example, the mainstream teacher presents the lesson and the English language teacher interjects examples, explanations, and extensions of key ideas. The English language teacher can provide strategies to facilitate content acquisition for the ELLs.

Source: Adapted from Friend and Cook (2003), Honigsfeld and Dove (2008).

(Hargreaves, 1994). This eliminates the absolute succeed-or-fail effect that both content and English language teachers can encounter when they are required to teach in isolation.

Teacher collaboration also enhances academic outcomes for ELLs. Recent research found a positive relationship between teacher collaboration and mathematics and reading achievement (Goddard, Goddard, & Tschannen-Moran, 2007). Finally, collaborative practices between English language teachers and content teachers can ensure that students' needs are better met than when students are in classrooms where language and content teachers do not co-teach (Honigsfeld & Dove, 2008).

How and When to Collaborate

Despite the benefits, teacher collaboration is not without its challenges. Research specifically looking at the barriers that English language and content teachers face when engaging in collaborative practices identified issues related to time, the culture of isolation, teacher positioning, and English language teachers' knowledge of content. Additionally, and importantly, positioning plays a role in successful teacher collaboration and co-teaching. Chapter 3 discussed research that found the co-teaching relationship to be the biggest barrier to successful CLIL (Mehisto, Marsh, & Frigols, 2008). Effective collaboration must start with a relationship in which both teachers are positioned equally; however, research shows that it is often evident that English language teachers are marginalized in some way, making meaningful collaboration ineffective. Such perceptions often reduce the English language educator to the status of helper rather than teacher. Recent work (DelliCarpini, 2009; DelliCarpini & Gulla, 2009) found that English language teachers feel that they are frequently not seen as real teachers by either their colleagues or their students and find themselves without classrooms (teaching in hallways or converted closets) and lacking resources.

So, collaboration is both promising and challenging, and when collaboration is enforced or imposed as a rigid and prescriptive approach, failure may be inevitable. Contextual factors (personalities, space, time, administrative support, etc.) play an important role in collaborative practice. If this continuum is presented as a menu of practices that teachers can select from, engaging in one or more concurrently or consecutively (see Table 7), the partnerships can have positive effects on both teachers and learners, which allows definition of collaboration where there is room for the weak form, the strong form, and a number of intermediate practices.

Where in the Curriculum Can Collaboration Occur?

There are natural starting places that allow English language teachers and content teachers to try various approaches and find something that works for them (see Table 7).

English language teachers and subject teachers can collaborate in a variety of flexible ways to engage in two-way CBI. We argue that this is different from traditional CBI in that it necessarily requires teachers to collaborate. Additionally, we believe that two-way CBI brings traditional CBI out of the language classroom, where it primarily exists, and into the mainstream, therefore making the language demands of the

Table 7. Elements of Collaboration in Two-Way CBI

Elements of collaboration	Where on the continuum
Curriculum: Building Background	
−Who are the ELLs? What are their backgrounds and experiences, and how may those impact instruction? −Share information about the context of the English language classroom and mainstream classroom −Discuss students' needs and interests −What are some challenges with the linguistic complexity of the language of the discipline?	−Informal discussions −Sharing resources −Classroom visits
Curriculum: Scaffolding Language and Content	
−Share key concepts −Share planned activities or co-plan activities −Modify objectives to meet the needs of the ELLs −Discuss ways to deconstruct the language of mathematics −Modify word problems −Select content and everyday vocabulary to focus on −Discuss linguistic features and complexities that need to be resolved −Select key content concepts −Select language functions critical to success with these key concepts −English language teachers and math teachers develop complementary language and content objectives	−Classroom visits −Sharing resources −Co-planning −Co-teaching
Curriculum: Assessment	
−Co-develop the classroom assessment plan −Content teacher can share mainstream assessments so the English language teachers can develop the linguistic skills needed for success within the context of the subject −English language teacher can work on assessment modifications, considerations, and criteria that are sensitive to the needs of ELLs	−Classroom visits −Sharing resources −Co-planning

content area a required topic of discussion, professional development, and focus at the teacher level.

Activity 4: Making Space for Collaboration

Using the information just presented, complete Table 8 with your colleague. We have included lesson elements as places to consider collaboration but have left space for you to include your own areas where collaboration could occur.

> ### REFLECTIVE BREAK
>
> - What is your experience with collaborative practices in the secondary-education setting? Have you received professional development and administrative support to engage in collaborative activities?
>
> - What barriers do you see to effective collaboration between subject teachers and English language teachers?
>
> - What would be the key elements for an educational program that wanted to develop a culture of collaboration?

Table 8. Collaboration Activity

Lesson element	Opportunity to collaborate	English language teacher's role	Subject teacher's role	Which model would suit this collaborative practice in your own setting?	Potential challenges or barriers	Ways to overcome the challenge or barrier
Building and activating prior knowledge						
Academic vocabulary development						
Academic literacy development						
Academic oral language development						
Concept development						
Academic writing development						
Assessment of language and content knowledge						

5

A Two-Way Approach

The Problem of Isolated CBI

Subject teachers should not be expected to become English language teachers, nor should English language teachers be expected to possess the subject knowledge that subject-area specialists have in fields outside of English language, linguistics, applied linguistics, and language pedagogy. As already stated, CBI usually happens in isolation (in the English language classroom and during sheltered instruction in the mainstream classroom). The problem with this model is that, for the most part, neither teacher is prepared to build skills outside of his or her respective discipline. We therefore look at two-way CBI as a necessary way of redefining traditional notions of CBI and expanding the work being done on teacher collaboration to develop an environment where teachers engage in mirror-image practice. In such an environment, the English language teacher focuses on language-driven CBI, and the subject teacher focuses on content-driven CBI through collaborative practices so the needs of ELLs are met by those most qualified to meet them in both settings.

How to Accomplish Two-Way CBI

The method of accomplishing this two-way CBI model is through engaging in collaborative practice, which results in complementary, co-developed objectives to be actualized in each classroom setting. We use the terms *content-driven language objectives* for the language classroom and *language-driven content objectives* in the subject-area classroom as a way to distinguish this approach. These objectives supplement the traditional content or language learning needs and objectives in each setting. This differs from traditional views in that, rather than having both teachers develop both sets of objectives (or only one teacher working in isolation), teachers conflate the academic language needs and the content needs into objectives that either make the language of the discipline visible in the content classroom or build the actual academic language needed for subject-area success in the language classroom.

We have found in our own practices as teacher-educators that content teachers frequently have very little knowledge or skill in developing language objectives that are different from what they would do for their native-speaking students. Although there may be some awareness of language, many objectives fail because they do not identify the language of the discipline that ELLs need to master for the particular content learning: They are too general, not measurable, or do not identify a specific language function (describe, define, analyze, argue, etc.) or how that language will be used in acquisition of the content material.

Conversely, English language teachers who have a background in language pedagogy, linguistics, and applied linguistics experience challenges in writing content objectives that really get to the heart of the content knowledge needed for academic success. Knowledge of the discipline is required to understand what content is important and how to focus on that content. Additionally, the connections between a current topic and the greater subject are critical for building a comprehensive understanding for students. Poorly written objectives for the English language classroom can be superficial in nature, can miss important connections between concepts, and can actually cause students to be confused when they enter their mainstream classroom if the English language teacher does not have a solid understanding of the discipline.

Developing Better CBI Objectives

All well-developed objectives share common characteristics: behavior, conditions, and criteria. Table 9 shows how these parts interact in a content-driven language objective.

Table 9. Objective Components

Characteristic	Description	Example
Behavior	What the students will be able to do as a result of the learning activities	Students will use comparatives (*big, bigger, biggest*) and superlatives (*more, most*) and the language of *greater than* and *less than*
Conditions	How the students will be able to do this	Orally, during the class discussion, and in writing while they solve word problems, students will be able to identify the < and > symbols and discuss the relationships between numbers and quantities of items (7 is *greater than* 3, 3 is *less than* 7; Sofia's allowance is *big*, Paloma's allowance is *bigger* than Sofia's, Oliver's is the *biggest* of all; Oliver's allowance is *greater than* Sofia's)
Criteria	The degree or level to which students are required to perform	With at least an 85% accuracy rate

The objective in Table 9 is clear, explicitly states what type of language is needed and how it will be used, and is measurable. It contains the performance (use comparatives, superlatives, and the language of *greater than* and *less than* when comparing numbers and quantities of items), the conditions (orally and in writing), and the criteria (with an 85% accuracy rate). The content knowledge cannot be developed without the development of the language. By having a clear, detailed, and measurable content-driven language objective, activities, vocabulary, and assessment flow naturally from the statement and allow teachers to design instruction that supports the stated objective.

Complementary Objectives: What Do They Look Like?

The following is a closer look at how complementary objectives can be collaboratively developed: Ms. Moran is a high-school math teacher. Mr. Everitt is the English language teacher in the same school. Eight of Mr. Everitt's English language students are in Ms. Moran's 6th period math class. Mr. Everitt and Ms. Moran have engaged in a number of collaborative practices, starting with informal discussions about shared students and finally engaging in co-planning. Ms. Moran has developed a unit of instruction on the properties of shapes. She decided to reinforce student knowledge on the classification of triangles and quadrilaterals because in previous years students had difficulty associating properties with well-defined triangle and quadrilateral types. Her reflections with Mr. Everitt on the causes of such problems led her to think that students had little understanding of how to classify and how to make abstractions from concrete representations of shapes to different concepts that arise from the classification criterion used. She found in the *Mathematics Teacher Journal* innovative activities that she could use to address these issues; however, she was afraid that her ELLs might have trouble with the commonly used terminology associated with different shapes and sought the opportunity to collaborate with Mr. Everitt because he could address the linguistic features surrounding the definitions of these concepts to activate students' prior knowledge.

Ms. Moran and Mr. Everitt decided to first plan complementary activities on the study of triangles, so students could use repetitive reasoning when moving to the more complex study of quadrilaterals.

Following is a collaboratively developed, content-driven language objective for the English language class (that makes the language of the discipline visible):

- Students will be able to (SWBAT) associate triangles with their names, during whole-group and small-group discussions, based on the length of their sides and on the measure of their angles using the following academic terminology: *sides(s), angle(s), length of a side, measure of an angle, base of an isosceles triangle, right angle, obtuse angle, acute angle, isosceles triangle, equilateral triangle, scalene triangle, right triangle, obtuse, triangle, acute triangle, equal, unequal, congruent, degree(s).*

- Additionally, students will be able to explain, using the academic vocabulary, conceptual hierarchical relationships among different kinds of triangles whenever they exist (*Is an equilateral triangle isosceles?*) as well as identify and communicate in written and oral forms different ways in which these could be defined as they use different classification criteria. Students will be able to identify all types of triangles with 100% accuracy, understand the linguistic functions related to classifications as they associate observable features of shapes with a classification criterion with 90% accuracy, and correctly define all types of triangles with 85% accuracy measured by their usage of Venn diagrams, concept mapping and other graphic organizers, and as they communicate their findings.

To successfully achieve these objectives, manipulatives (triangle-shaped objects) will be provided, students will work in small groups to name the types of triangles, and they will be required to justify why they classified the particular triangles as they did and in written form, using the academic vocabulary of the characteristics of the triangles. They will present their findings and justifications to the whole group. Then additional discussion, using the academic language, can ensue that challenges or further clarifies the initial classifications the students made.

During the discussion, a list of different types of triangles is generated and displayed in a graphic organizer (see Figure 2).

Students will discover that they have learned that sometimes triangles are classified by the length of their sides or, separately, by the characteristics of their angles. Now they have a system that conflates these two different systems into one, therefore containing all salient features (side length and angle measure) in one system; for example, an isosceles triangle can be either obtuse, right, or acute and scalene triangles may as well. The students will be asked to develop two graphic organizers, one making use of the side length and the other making use of angle measure, which defines angle type (obtuse, right, acute). Expected responses would look like Figures 3 and 4.

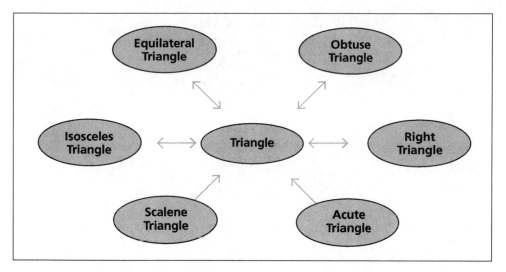

Figure 2. Graphic Organizer of Triangle Types

Using the two-way CBI model, the English language teacher would develop the objective of triangle classification in collaboration with the math teacher (to make the content needed visible) and the math teacher, in collaboration with the English language teacher, would

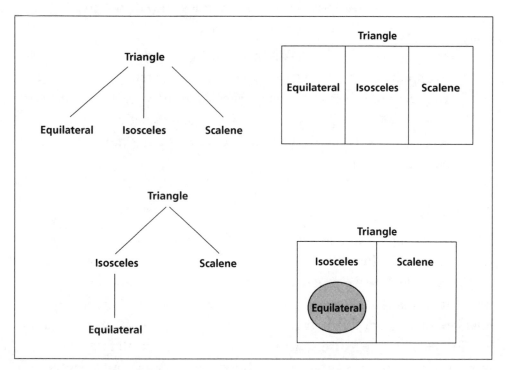

Figure 3. Side Length Patterns

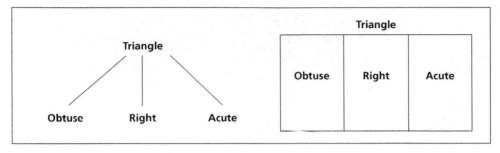

Figure 4. Angle Type

create the following complementary language-driven content objectives for the mainstream lesson:

- Students will be able to discuss triangle classification using the following sentence starter: Triangle ABC is a (an) _____ triangle because _____ of its angle measures are _____. Students will generate sentences using a classification table (partition–pairs classification) and/or triangle names, which can act as a semantic feature analysis chart to develop dictionary-like definitions (Alonso & Malkevitch, 2013) using correct prepositions, conjunctions, and direct and indirect articles with an 80% level of accuracy.

- Students will be able to discuss, during whole-group and small-group discussions, their arguments and constructively analyze the arguments of others using the academic vocabulary through oral presentation of their cooperative group activity results with an 80% level of accuracy, measured by the table and the sentences generated.

Two-Way CBI in Action

Ms. Moran, the math teacher, and Mr. Everitt, the English language teacher, further illustrate what effective two-way CBI can look like and how collaborative practices enhance student learning in both the content and language classrooms. These teachers have decided to co-plan a two-period lesson around a classroom activity on percentage increase and decrease to re-teach what they have already covered in their classes on this topic. They choose to work around a problem from Tannenbaum's (2010) book, which contains many of the linguistic complexities already discussed here and will help students to learn how to calculate the best price for a special item. The original problem is

A toy store buys a certain toy from the distributor to sell during the Christmas season. The store marks up the price of the toy by 80% (the intended profit margin). Unfortunately for the toy store, the toy is a bust and doesn't sell well. After Christmas, it goes on sale for 40% off the marked price. After a while, an additional 25% markdown is taken off the sale price, and the toy is put on the clearance table. With all the markups and markdowns, what is the percentage profit/loss to the toy store? (p. 366)

Both Mr. Everitt and Ms. Moran agreed that the level of generality of the problem was high, so they decided that assigning a number to the given cost [C = $100] would be clearer and would allow students to find a starting point for problem solving. As students were able to understand that the operations performed on [C] were independent of its value, Ms. Moran could guide them towards the generalization. As Ms. Moran explained the math to Mr. Everitt, he suggested that a timeline would help their ELLs visualize the changes in the price of the item overtime (see Figure 5). In addition, they collaboratively worked to deconstruct the linguistic complexities of the problem for the math lesson and to develop content-driven and language-driven objectives for both classes as well as activities and assessments that help students to meet the developed objectives.

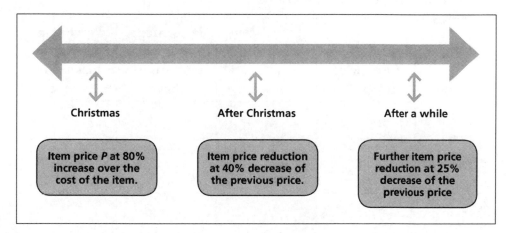

Figure 5. Timeline for Classroom Activity on Percentages

In deconstructing the linguistic complexity of the word problem, Mr. Everitt codes the issues he finds: **bold** for cultural issues that may cause misunderstanding, underlined for general linguistic issues (low-frequency vocabulary, grammatical structures, etc.), and *italic* for mathematical terms:

A toy store buys a certain toy from the distributor to sell during the **Christmas season**. The store marks up the price of the toy *by* 80% (the intended *profit margin*). Unfortunately, for the toy store, the toy is a bust and doesn't sell well. After Christmas, it goes on sale for **40% off the marked price**. After a while, an additional 25% **markdown** is taken off the **sale price** and the toy is put on the clearance table. With all the **markups and markdowns**, what is the **percentage profit/loss** to the toy store?

Mr. Everitt develops a table for students to fill in after he engages in a guided reading of the problem (see Table 10).

Mr. Everitt focuses on having the students fill in the shaded areas in his English language class. They then take their partially completed charts to Ms. Moran's class and begin solving the math problem. The result of the two-way CBI model is that students have a seamless integration of both content and language, and English language teachers and mainstream teachers are collaborating to ensure this integration.

Table 10. Word Problem Deconstruction

Time	Item price (toy price)	Is the item marked up or marked down?	Percentage of the mark up or mark down	Percentage of profit or loss to the store
Christmas season				
After Christmas				
After a while				

Activity 5

Referring to the preceding problem, identify the features on Table 11 for both the content and English language classroom. Then, in Table 12, develop complementary objectives for each classroom.

Effective two-way CBI begins with effective collaborative partnerships. Teachers can begin by engaging in one or more of the collaborative practices discussed. Remember that collaboration is not a one-size-fits-all endeavor, and different teaching contexts call for different types of collaborative practices. Additionally, teachers should feel free to flexibly select and modify these practices based on their unique situations. For example, collaboration can start with informal discussions about shared students, lead to classroom visits to observe each other's practice, and develop into co-planning but may never reach the co-teaching stage. This is fine because the success of these partnerships

Table 11. Features Identification Activity

Feature	Content classroom	English language classroom
Key content concept		
Key vocabulary		
Language functions and skills		

Table 12. Complementary Objectives

Two-way CBI complementary objective	
Math classroom	English language classroom
Language-driven content objectives:	Content-driven language objectives:

partially lies in the flexibility and the bottom-up development (teachers making decisions about how and when to collaborate) rather than top-down mandates.

Perhaps the most important elements in developing effective two-way CBI activities are discussion between teachers and co-planning. Although flexibility in collaborative practices enhances outcomes, it is critical to have discussions about the language of the discipline and the academic language needs of ELLs for true academic success. What emerges from these shared discussions and co-planning activities, as evident with Mr. Everitt and Ms. Moran, are truly integrated content and language learning that have the following features:

- Language and content skills are built in both settings.
- The language of the discipline is made visible in the content setting.
- The actual academic language skills are built in the language setting, using the same topic, materials, and problems encountered in the content classroom.
- Teachers from both disciplines gain an understanding of the needs of ELLs in both settings.
- Assessment activities flow naturally from the collaboratively developed complementary objectives because objectives are written to include measurable performance criteria connected to both language and content outcomes.

Finally, anticipating challenges through reflective practice, reflective discussion, and developing critical partnerships can help teachers avoid the natural problems that will arise. Teachers can problematize (based on their own experiences, content knowledge, and pedagogical knowledge) the issues that students will encounter with the language of the content (English language teacher sharing with the content teacher), the content itself (content teacher sharing with the English language teacher), and the collaborative partnership (barriers to effective collaboration, logistics, negotiation of issues).

Successful integration of language and content has the potential to create successful learning environments for ELLs through the meaningful acquisition of the academic subject under investigation and the academic language needed to communicate effectively within that subject. Both English language and content teachers face challenges in understanding and implementing CBI effectively. Students whose L1 is not English who are engaged in academic learning in English-medium programs are a growing part of the educational landscape. Two-way CBI enables both subject and language teachers to focus on the required language and skills to help students succeed in these settings. When teachers are prepared to teach all learners they encounter in their classrooms, all students' educational success and attainment are raised.

6

Conclusion

In this book, we described an expanded approach to both CBI and teacher collaboration. With increasing populations of ELLs, as well as growing numbers of English-medium schools, it is critical that English language teachers and content teachers engage in collaborative practices that build the types of academic learning ELLs need to be successful in the content setting. We focus on math activities as our examples in this book because math is one of the areas where the academic achievement gap is widest, yet people commonly believe that math is a universal language and that ELLs do not need special help. The achievement data, both in terms of success for secondary-level students and the rate of scholarly publications in English (the dominant language of academic publishing), suggest otherwise. Although CBI is a promising practice, it usually takes place in isolation, in the English language setting. When teachers focus on collaboration, they can take CBI out of the language classroom and move toward a two-way CBI approach, where content teachers and English language teachers work together to develop complementary content-driven (taught in the language classroom) and language-driven (taught in the content classroom) CBI language and content objectives. We present collaboration as a continuum of activities so that teachers can be flexible in the types of practices they engage in, depending on their individual contextual factors as well as those collaborative practices. With this flexibility, teachers can create a framework within which to develop two-way CBI objectives.

References

Alonso, O. B., & Malkevitch, J. (2013). Classifying triangles and quadrilaterals. *Mathematics Teacher*, *106*(7), 541–547.

Brandt, C. (2010). Scaffolding ESL undergraduates' academic acculturation through journal articles as teaching resource. *International Journal of Arts and Sciences*, *3*(17), 276–286.

Brinton, D. M., Snow, M. A., & Wesche, M. B. (1989). *Content-based second language instruction*. Boston, MA: Heinle and Heinle.

Coleman, J. A. (2006). English-medium teaching in European higher education. *Language Teaching*, *39*(1), 1–14.

Crandall, J., & Tucker, R. G. (1990). Content-based instruction in second and foreign languages. In A. Padilla, H. Fairchild, & C. Valadez (Eds.), *Foreign language education: Issues and strategies* (pp. 187–200). Newbury Park, CA: Sage.

de Jong, E. J., & Harper, C. A. (2005). Preparing mainstream teachers for English language learners: Is being a good teacher good enough? *Teacher Education Quarterly*, *32*(2), 101–124.

DelliCarpini, M. (2009). Dialogues across disciplines: Preparing ESL teachers for interdisciplinary collaboration. *Current Issues in Education*, *11*(2). Retrieved from http://cie.asu.edu/volume11/index.html

DelliCarpini, M., & Gulla, A. N. (2009). Creating space for collaboration. *English Journal*, *98*(4), 133–137.

Derwing, T. M., DeCorby, E., Ichikawa, J., & Jamieson, K. (1999). Some factors that affect the success of ESL high school students. *The Canadian Modern Language Review*, *55*(4), 532–547.

Friend, M., & Cook, L. (2003). *Interactions: Collaboration skills for school professionals* (4th ed.). New York, NY: Longman.

Fry, R. (2007). How far behind in math and reading are English language learners? Pew Hispanic Center Report. Washington, DC: Pew Hispanic Center.

Genesee, F. (2004). What do we know about bilingual education for majority language students? In T. K. Bhatia & W. Ritchie (Eds.), *Handbook of bilingualism and multiculturalism* (pp. 547–576). Malden, MA: Blackwell.

Goddard, Y. L., Goddard, R. D., & Tschannen-Moran, M. (2007). A theoretical and empirical investigation of teacher collaboration for school improvement and student achievement in public elementary schools. *Teachers College Record, 109*(4), 877–896.

Grabe, W., & Stoller, F. L. (1997). Content-based instruction: Research foundations. In M. A. Snow & D. M. Brinton (Eds.), *The content-based classroom: Perspectives on integrating language and content* (pp. 5–21). White Plains, NY: Longman.

Graddol, D. (2007). *English next.* London, England: The British Council. Retrieved from http://www.britishcouncil.org/learning-research-english -next.pdf.

Hargreaves, A. (1994) *Changing teachers, changing times: Teachers' work and culture in the postmodern age.* London, England: Cassell.

Herrera, S. G., & Murray, K. G. (2005). *Mastering ESL and bilingual methods: Differentiated instruction for culturally and linguistically diverse (CLD) students.* New York, NY: Pearson Education.

Honigsfeld, A., & Dove, M. (2008). Co-teaching in the ESL classroom. *Delta Kappa Gamma Bulletin, 74*(2), 8–14.

King, D. (2004). The scientific impact of nations. *Nature, 430,* 311–316.

Man, J. P., Weinkaif, J. G., Tsang, M., & Sin, D. D. (2004). Why do some countries publish more than others? An international comparison of research funding, English proficiency and publication output in highly ranked general medical journals. *European Journal of Epidemiology, 19,* 811–817.

Martiniello, M. (2008). Linguistic complexity, schematic representations, and differential item functioning for English language learners in math tests. *Harvard Educational Review, 78*(2), 160–179.

Mauranen, A. (2003). The corpus of English as lingua franca in academic settings. *TESOL Quarterly, 37*(3), 513–527.

McGloin, M. (2011). *An achievement gap revealed: A mixed method research investigation of Canadian-born English language learners* (Unpublished thesis). Ontario Institute for Studies in Education, University of Toronto, Canada.

Mehisto, P. (2008). CLIL counterweights: Recognising and decreasing disjuncture in CLIL. *International CLIL Research Journal, 1*(1), 93–119.

Mehisto, P., Marsh, D., & Frigols, M. J. (2008). *Uncovering CLIL: Content and language integrated learning in bilingual and multilingual education.* Oxford, England: Macmillan.

Met, M. (1999). Curriculum decision-making in content-based language teaching. In J. Cenoz & F. Genesee (Eds.), *Beyond bilingualism: Multilingualism and multilingual education* (pp. 35–63). Clevedon, England: Multilingual Matters.

National Center for Educational Statistics. (2002). *Schools and staffing survey, 1999–2000: Overview of the data for public, private, public charter, and Bureau of Indian Affairs elementary and secondary schools.* Washington, DC: NCES.

Short, D., Echevarría, J., & Richards-Tutor, C. (2011). Research on academic literacy development in sheltered instruction classrooms. *Language Teaching Research, 15*(3), 363–380.

Snow, M. A. (1998). Trends and issues in content-based instruction. *Annual Review of Applied Linguistics, 18*, 243–267.

Tannenbaum, P. (2010). *Excursions in modern mathematics* (7th ed.). New York, NY: Prentice Hall.

TESOL International Association. (2008). Position statement on teacher preparation for content-based instruction (CBI). Available from http://www.tesol.org/docs/pdf/10882.pdf?sfvrsn=2

Toronto District School Board. (2008). Students at risk: Our children our schools. Retrieved from http://www.tdsb.on.ca/

Also Available in the English Language Teacher Development Series

Reflective Teaching (Thomas S. C. Farrell)

Teaching Listening (Ekaterina Nemtchinova)

Teaching Pronunciation (John Murphy)

Language Classroom Assessment (Liying Cheng)

Cooperative Learning and Teaching (George Jacobs & Harumi Kimura)

Classroom Research for Language Teachers (Tim Stewart)

Teaching Digital Literacies (Joel Bloch)

Teaching Reading (Richard Day)

Teaching Grammar (William Crawford)

Teaching Vocabulary (Michael Lessard-Clouston)

Teaching Writing (Zuzana Tomas, Ilka Kostka, & Jennifer A. Mott-Smith)

English Language Teachers as Administrators (Dan Tannacito)

Content-Based Instruction (Margo Dellicarpini & Orlando Alonso)

Teaching English as an International Language
(Ali Fuad Selvi & Bedrettin Yazan)

Teaching Speaking (Tasha Bleistein, Melissa K. Smith, & Marilyn Lewis)

www.tesol.org/bookstore
tesolpubs@brightkey.net
Request a copy for review
Request a Distributor Policy